Shakespeare and the Ulster Dialect

SHAKESPEARE AND THE ULSTER DIALECT

S<small>IR</small> J<small>OHN</small> W<small>ILLIAM</small> B<small>YERS</small>

B<small>OOKS</small> U<small>LSTER</small>

First published in the *Northern Whig*, Belfast, 22nd April, 1916.

This new edition published in 2014

Typographical arrangement, design, layout
© Books Ulster

All rights reserved. No part of this publication may be reproduced, stored in a retrieval system, or transmitted by any means, electronic, mechanical, photocopying or otherwise, without the prior permission of the publisher.

ISBN 978-1-910375-00-6

SHAKESPEARE AND THE ULSTER DIALECT.

By SIR JOHN BYERS, M.A., M.D.,

President (1915-1916) of the Belfast Literary Society.

Of the various important elements (Celtic, English, Scotch, and French) which when combined form the Ulster dialect one of the most interesting component parts is that which the settlers from England brought with them. A few years (1603-1605) before the period of the great Plantation of Ulster (1609-1610), but centuries after the arrival of the Anglo-Normans in Lecale, County Down, under Sir John de Courci in 1177—when Henry II. was King—Englishmen had settled in parts of West Down whose native places were Lancashire and Cheshire, while others, who came from Devonshire, Lancashire, and Cheshire, went to reside in Monaghan and South Antrim. At the time of what is termed the great Plantation of Ulster, in the reign of James I., at the beginning of the seventeenth century (1609-1610), Englishmen came also from Lancashire and Cheshire, but the great majority journeyed from the apple districts of Warwickshire, Worcestershire, and Gloucestershire, from Nottinghamshire, and even from as far south as London, one of the most important features of

the scheme being the settlement of what was then
called the County of Coleraine (afterwards named
Londonderry) by the Corporation and twelve Guilds
of the City of London. This great

English Immigration

commenced on the two sides of Belfast, on the west at
Carrickfergus (which had a reputation and a name
as an assize town centuries before Belfast existed),
and on the east at Ballymacarrett. These settlers
absorbed Belfast, which at first, like Derry, became
largely English. Advancing up the fertile valley of
the River Lagan, these English immigrants settled in
Lisburn (where the famous preacher Jeremy Taylor,
who was appointed Bishop of Down and Connor in
1660, died in 1667). A portion of them passed on to
Hillsborough, Dromore (the only town in the North
of Ireland with the stocks, a mode of punishment
for petty offences which existed from Anglo-Saxon
times down to the nineteenth century—it was
used in Rugby in 1865—and to which Shakespeare
frequently refers, as, for example, "Fetch forth
the stocks," in "King Lear," II., ii., 122; and where
Thomas Percy, who edited the "Reliques of Ancient
English Poetry," which contains old English ballads
and some beautiful lyrics of the Elizabethan age, in
1765, and who was appointed Bishop of Dromore in
1782, lies buried in the Cathedral beside his wife, the
heroine of the famous song written by her husband,
"O Nancy, wilt thou go with me?"), Banbridge,

Shakespeare and the Ulster Dialect

Newry, and Hilltown. The greater number of the English immigrants extended along the side of Lough Neagh to Lurgan, Portadown, Armagh (the oldest city in Ireland, full of historical, ecclesiastical, and academic traditions), and right away to the mountains of Tyrone, and on to Fermanagh and Cavan. The large area which these settlers occupied was at first markedly English, and even now,

After an Interval of Three Centuries,

as you motor through parts of it the very trees—sycamore, apple, and elm—the famous orchards (County Armagh has been called "The Orchard of Ireland") in the vicinity of Portadown, Richhill, and Loughgall, the size of the farms, and the type of many of the homesteads all indicate the source of the people who came originally from England.

While the early Anglo-Normans carried with them some mediaeval English words (in my class-roll at Queen's University there are frequently Anglo-Norman surnames), it was the English immigrants who came in such large numbers at the time of the great Plantation who brought with them to Ulster the current English of the time of Queen Elizabeth (1533-1603)—the period of the later Renaissance of art and letters—and especially the words and phrases found in the works of Shakespeare (1564-1616), the foremost writer in English literature. It is a remarkable fact that many of the very words and phrases used by Shakespeare, and which have since largely been lost, are still found in the dialect of his native Warwickshire and the surrounding counties; and as it was from these districts that so many of the English colonists came to Ulster at the time of the great Plantation a large number of these words and phrases are still found in our dialect. Indeed, nowhere in the British Empire are there still in existence so many of Shakespeare's words—not now known (or very rare) in other places—as in the Midland Counties of England, taking Warwickshire as the centre, and in the North of Ireland. As Mrs. Wright has pointed out in her "Rustic Speech and Folk-lore," some of these words and phrases were at Shakespeare's time part and parcel of the standard vocabulary, and might be put by Shakespeare into the mouths of the highest personages; others, again, might even then have been regarded by him as dialect and natural only to the speech of the people. Until the end of the eighteenth century there was

A Tradition in Ulster

that pure English was spoken in Lisburn, and it was computed less than half a century ago—1878—that, while at that date a glossary of more than 2,000 words would be required to enable a modern Englishman to read his Shakespeare, probably about 200 words (one in ten) or less, would be all that an intelligent North of Ireland person would need to understand the works of the greatest of poets and dramatists. This circumstance is all the more remarkable when

Shakespeare and the Ulster Dialect

it is recollected that Shakespeare's vocabulary exceeds both in amount and variety that of any other writer; indeed, one of the many unsolved riddles in connection with the famous dramatist is how he managed to acquire that precise and accurate knowledge of the details of so many occupations as are referred to in his works. Many of the so-called "vulgarisms" met with in the spoken language—or dialect—of the people of the North of Ireland belong to the Augustan age of English literature, and have come down from the period of Queen Elizabeth through the English planters. These people, having once acquired the vernacular English of that wonderful time, have fortunately handed it down through their descendants as a spoken language, despite the absurd attempts of some pedants to stamp it out, and as a result this vigorous English, with its supposed "vulgarisms," which Sidney (1554-1586), Spenser (1552-1599)—the "poet's poet"—Kyd (1557-1595), Bacon (1561-1626), Ben Jonson (1573-1637), Marlowe (1564-1593), and, above all, Shakespeare (1564-1616) employed so well, has added greatly to the recognised force, the crisp clearness, and the subtle humour of the Ulster dialect.

ILLUSTRATIONS.

The following Ulster dialect words and expressions, with their Shakespearean equivalents, will illustrate and emphasise what I have written. Limited space prevents me giving many more examples which I have collected. On points of philology and dialect I have taken the Oxford and Dialect Dictionaries as among the acknowledged authorities:—

"A," used before numerals and nouns of multitude, is common all over the North of Ireland, as "A good few voted against it," "There wasn't a one of them at the meeting." Compare "Macbeth," III., iv., 156—

"There's not a one of them, but in his house I keep a servant fee'd,"

and "King John," IV., ii., 199—

"A many thousand warlike French."

"Afeard" or "feard," frightened.—"Don't be afeard of the dog; he's harmless." Compare "A Midsummer Night's Dream," III., i., 25—

"Will not the ladies be afeard of the lion?"

This word "afeard," which is rare in literature after 1700 (being supplanted by "afraid"), Shakespeare uses more than thirty times in his plays.

"Affright," to frighten.—"Did I affright ye?" a remark made by one person on suddenly meeting another on a dark night. (I heard it used recently by a native of County Cavan.) This word "affright" as a verb, employed in a transitive sense to frighten, is now archaic. It probably was formed from the pre-existing affright, the past participle of the old English afyrhtan, from a, pref., i intensive, and fyrhtan, to frighten. The doubling of the "f" is analogous to forms like af-firm, af-fix, from the Latin "ad." This use of affright has been long obsolete, and a later form was affrighted, meaning alarmed, frightened. It also is met in Ulster, as when a mother says to her child who runs, crying to her, from a dog, "Were ye affrighted?" Compare "King Henry VI.," Part I., I., iv., 43—

"Here, said they, is the terror of the French,
The scarecrow that affrights our children so,"

and "Othello," V., ii., 100—

"And that th' affrighted Globe
Did yawne at Alteration."

"Alablaster."—Throughout the North of Ireland alablaster is used for a fine variety of carbonate or sulphate of lime. I have heard a sick person's face described as being "as white as alablaster." Alablaster is the sixteenth and seventeenth century spelling of the modern alabaster. Some think the "bl" is due to a sense-association with "bleach," "blanch," and other "bl" forms indicating whiteness; but this old spelling may have arisen owing to a confusion with "arblaster," a crossbowman, also written "alablaster." The word is derived from the old French "alabastre" (modern French "albâtre"), an adaptation from the Latin "alabaster," -trum, from the Greek "alabastros" or "alabastos," said to be from a town in Egypt. Compare "The Merchant of Venice," I., i., 84—

"Why should a man whose blood is warm within
Sit like his grandsire cut in alablaster?"

"Alablaster" is no mere vulgar or corrupt misspelling or mispronunciation, but a genuine old form

Preserved in the Ulster Dialect

(like such similar archaic forms as crowner, laylock, disgest, flannen, lew-warm, ax, afeard), and which was once used under the distinguished patronage of Sidney in his "Arcadia," and of Shakespeare in five of his works.

"Prisoners' Base or Bars."—When I was a pupil at the Royal Academical Institution, Belfast, this was a popular game, which, according to Strutt in his "Sports and Pastimes," dates back to Edward III. Base is used specifically for the "goal," "base," or "home," or it may be a phonetic corruption of "bars," the enclosure or camp "barred" off. Compare "Cymbeline," V., iii., 20—

"Athwart the lane,
    He with two striplings—lads more like to run

Shakespeare and the Ulster Dialect

The country base than to commit such slaughter—
Made good the passage."

The game is referred to in Spenser's "Faerie Queen."

"Bottle," "bottling," "to bottle."
(1) Substantive—a bundle of hay or straw.
(2) Verb.—To make hay or straw into bundles.
"Give that horse a bottle of hay."
"What are the men doin' in the barn?" "Bottlin' straw."
"When are you goin' to bottle that thrashed straw?"

Bottle is from the old French botel, diminutive of bot, masculine form of botte, a bundle. There is also an Anglo-Norman botel, "botte de foin," and boteler, to make into bundles or bottles. We have in Chaucer (1386)—

"He shal telle a tale, by my fey!
Although it be nat worth a botel hey,"

and the old saying, "To look for a needle in a bottle of hay" (or "straw"), is as old as 1655 (Clarke. "Phras. Puer.") Compare "A Midsummer-Night's Dream," IV., i., 30, where Bottom in reply to Titania says, "Methinks I have a great desire to a bottle of hay."

"Bottle," "bottling," and "to bottle" are found all over the North of Ireland.

An Ulster child, while moving four of the fingers of the two interlocked hands, will say—

"Two men thrashin',
A wee bird pickin',
An' an old man bottlin' straw."

"Bugles" are used in Ulster for beads of any kind, as one girl looking at another's neck will say, "Where did you get the purty bugles ye'r wearin'?" In this sense Shakespeare uses the word twice. Compare "A Winter's Tale," IV., iv., 224—

"Bugle bracelet, necklace amber,
Perfume for a lady's chamber,"

and "As You Like It," III., v., 47—

"'Tis not your inky brows, your black silk hair,
Your bugle eyeballs, nor your cheek of cream
That can entame my spirits to your worship."

In certain parts of Ulster "bugle" is used in a more restricted sense for a tube-shaped, or elongated, glass-bead.

"Beneficial," useful, advantageous.—"I suppose you fine (find) yer motor car beneficial." Compare "Othello," II., ii., 7—

"For, besides these beneficial news, it is the celebration of his nuptial."

"Brave," "Brave and," "Bravely."— "That's a brave

Shakespeare and the Ulster Dialect

day" is a phrase which means in Ulster simply that it is a good day. "You're brave and early," "He's a brave wee fella," "Taties are brave and chape," "He's doin' bravely," "He's brave (or quare) and fear'd" (said of a frightened child) are expressions often heard in the North of Ireland, but the word "brave" as here used conveys no military sense. Compare Sonnet 12, 2—

"See the brave day sunk in hideous night,"

and "As You Like It," III., iv., 39—

"O that's a brave man,
He writes brave verses, speaks brave words, swears brave oaths,"

and "Troilus and Cressida," I., ii., 198—

"Here's an excellent place; here we may see most bravely."

In Ulster a patient who is "bad with the bravelies" will soon be well.

"Bum-Bailey," a contemptuous term applied to a sheriff's officer or bailiff who served writs and often made arrests or prosecutions. It was sometimes applied in contempt to a "bog-bailiff," who was an important official who parcelled out "bog" or "moss," for cutting turf, to the tenants. In contempt such a person would be styled "an oul' bum-bailiff" or "an oul' bog-bum-bailey." Shakespeare employs the word only once, and that is in "Twelfth Night," III., iv., 194—

"Go, Sir Andrew; scout me for him at the corner of the orchard, like a bum-bailie."

"Child" or "Chile," a female infant.— "Is that a chile or a boy yer nursing?" Compare "A Winter's Tale," III., iii., 71—

"Mercy on's, a barne; a very pretty barne! A boy or a child, I wonder?"

"Char," "Charring," "Char-woman."—"What does that woman do?" "She chars," or "She goes out charring," or "She is a charwoman," or "She knocks out a livin' charring"—that is, she is a woman who, generally in towns, does odd jobs or turns of housework. (Char, or chare, is from the old English cerr, cerran, a turn.) Compare "Anthony and Cleopatra," IV., xv., 75—

"The maid that milks
And does the meanest chares" (turns of work).

In the United States

the phonetic variant of char is chore, so Emerson writes "Let us live in corners and do chores."

Shakespeare and the Ulster Dialect

"Colley" or "Colly," dirt, smut, soot, coal-dust.—"Close that window and keep the colley out," "The clothes on the line are covered with colley," "Go, boy, an' wash that colley off yer face." It is the same word as the sixteenth-century colie, coaly, an adjective, meaning dirtied with coal-dust or soot; or it may be a dialect form of the substantive collow, soot, smut, coal-dust, from the old English colgian, from colig, coaly, from col, coal. Compare "A Midsummer Night's Dream," I., i., 145—

"Brief as the lightning in the collied night"

(blackened or literally smutted with coal). Shakespeare found the word in Staffordshire, where it is still existent in the dialect of the colliers. In "Othello," II., iii., 185, the word is used figuratively in the sense of obscured or darkened—

"And passion, having my best judgment collied,
Assays to lead the way."

When two young people of opposite sexes are seen talking intimately, or, as it is said, "colloguing," someone will observe, "They are colley-washing," a remark which recalls the famous scene in Sterne's "Tristram Shandy," when the Widow Wadman, holding up her cambric handkerchief to her left eye as she approached the door of Uncle Toby's sentry-box, said, "I am half-distracted, Captain Shandy, a mote or sand or something—I know not what—has got into this eye of mine. Do look into it; it is not in the white."

"Crowner," coroner.—"The crowner's goin' to hold an inquest the morra" (tomorrow). Compare "Hamlet," V., i., 4—

> "The crowner hath sate on her
> And finds it Christian burial,"

and V.. i., 24—

> "Crowners-quest law."

"Disgest," "Disgist," "Indisgestion."—A doctor will often hear that a patient "can't disgest (disgist) his food," or that he or she is suffering from "indisgestion." The word "disgest" was common in the sixteenth and seventeenth centuries. It is now

A Dialectal Survival.

Compare "Julius Cæsar," I., ii., 305—

> "This rudeness is a sauce to his good wit,
>   Which gives men stomach to disgest (old editions)
>   his words with better appetite."

"Dry," thirsty.—"I'm very dry that hot day; God bless yer cows," was the expression used by a man who wanted some milk to quench his thirst.

Shakespeare and the Ulster Dialect

A "dry bargain," "dry talk." and "not water dry" are expressions that convey a hidden but obvious meaning. Compare "I. Henry IV.," I., iii., 31—

"When I was dry with rage and extreme toil,
Breathless and faint,"

and "Taming of the Shrew," V., ii., 143—

"A woman mov'd is like a fountain troubled,
Muddy, ill-seeming, thick, bereft of beauty;
And while it is so, none so dry or thirsty
Will deign to sip or touch one drop of it."

"Dun," a dull-brown or dull grey-brown colour, like the hair of the ass or mouse. "Who owes that dun mare?" is a phrase often heard in the Moy or the Saintfield horse fair. Two Ulstermen in a railway waiting-room carried on this dialogue, which I overheard:—"William, yer coat's gettin' a dun colour," to which his friend, unconsciously employing the literary mode of play on words so much liked by the Elizabethan writers, rejoined, "I (yes) it wos dun-coloured last year, but its clane (clean) done now." What a close parallel is found in "Romeo and Juliet" (I., iv., 40), when, in reply to the hero's words, "The game was ne'er so fair, and I am done," Mercutio replies—

"Tut, dun's the mouse, the constable's own word:
If thou art dun we'll draw thee from the mire

Shakespeare and the Ulster Dialect

Of this, Sir Reverence, love, wherein thou stick'st up to the ears!"

"Dun's the mouse" is a phrase alluding to the colour of the mouse. Compare with it the Ulster saying, "That's a dunduckity colour, like a mouse" (an undecided type of colour).

"Eternal," an expletive used like infernal to express abhorrence. "He's an eternal rascal." Compare "Othello," IV., ii., 130—

"I will be hang'd if some eternal villain
Have not devised this slander,"

and "Julius Caesar," I., ii., 160—

"The eternal devil."

"Favour," verb, to resemble, and substantive (a) grace, beauty of appearance, (b) permission, as something conceded through kindness or love. "That chile's sib to its father, but favours his mother," "Kissing goes by favour" (a play upon the two meanings of the substantive). Compare "Hamlet," IV., v., 168—

"Thought and affliction, passion, hell itself,
She turns to favour and to prettiness,"

and "Macbeth," I., iii., 61—

"Speak then to me who neither beg nor fear
Your favour nor you hate,"

and "As You Like It," IV., iii., 85—

"The boy is fair,
Of female favour."

In the modern dialect of Staffordshire favour is used, as in Ulster, for family likeness. "He favours his father's side of the house" is an expression

Often Heard in the North of Ireland.

"Handketcher," "Handkercher," and "Kerchief," handkerchief.—"Watch, chile, or ye'll loss yer handketcher." (Hand and middle English curchef and kerchef, shortened forms of coverchef and keverchef, from old French couvrechief, cuevrechief—couvrir, cover, and chief, head, from Latin caput.) Handkercher was common in literary use in the sixteenth and seventeenth centuries, and for long remained the spoken form. Compare "Henry V.," III., ii., 52—

"They would make me as familiar with men's pockets as their gloves or their handkerchers."

Originally the handkerchief was a square piece of cloth used as a covering for the head. There is a well-known game, "the handkercher game," played by Ulster children.

"Hold" or "Houl," to wager or bet.— "I'll houl ye a sovereign ye'll not do that again." Compare "Taming of the Shrew," III., ii., 79—

"I hold you a penny."

"Hangin' and Marriage."—"A dacent (decent) hangin' is no worse nor (than) a bad marriage" (Ulster phrase). Compare "Twelfth Night," I., v., 18—

"A good hanging prevents a bad marriage."

"I," an affirmative answer to a question as opposed to "No." "Do you hear what I'm saying?" "I." In Shakespeare's time "I" was commonly spoken and written for "Aye" (yes), which is now obsolete except in nautical language, when on board a ship the sailors reply, "Aye, aye, sir!" to the command of a superior officer as an indication that they hear and comprehend it, or, as in the House of Commons, when the Speaker in declaring that the affirmative voters are in a majority employs the quaint expression "The ayes have it." At first "Aye" was always written "I," as in "Romeo and Juliet," III., ii., 36, when the heroine says to the nurse—

"Hath Romeo slain himself? Say that but 'I,'
 And that bare vowel 'I' shall poison more
 Than the death-darting eye of cockatrice:
 I am not I, if there be such an 'I;'

Or these eyes shut, that make thee answer 'I.'
If he be slain say—'I,' or if not 'No:'
Brief sounds determine of my weal or woe."

"Kibe," "Kibes," "Kibey-heel," a sore or chapped heel, often the outcome of chilblains. Quite recently a boy came to the extern department of the Royal Victoria Hospital, Belfast, complaining that he had "kibey-heels." (Skeat thought the word kibe was connected with the Welsh "Cibi" (y gibi), a kibe.) The word kibe, a broken heel, is known in many parts of Ulster. Compare "Hamlet," V., i., 153—

"The toe of the peasant comes so near the heels of our courtier he galls his kibe,"

and "Tempest," II., i., 276—

"If, 'twere a kibe
'Twould put me to my slipper."

In the North of Ireland there are for this complaint two folk-cures.

In County Antrim

those affected with kibes get rid of the disease by going at night to a house and knocking loudly at the door. When the owner of the place calls out, "Who's there?" those knocking run away exclaiming, "Kiby heels, take that." As a result it is believed that the disease leaves the person affected and is transferred to the one who called "Who's there?" The other charm is to cover the kibes with gunpowder, after which a lighted match is applied.

"Insense," to cause a person to know something.—"I can't insense it into him." Compare "Henry VIII.," V., i., 43—

"I have insensed the Lords o' the Council that he is a most arch heretic."

This use of the word still exists in Staffordshire and Warwickshire. Since the seventeenth century the word is mainly dialectical.

"Inkle," "Inkle-weaver," "Beggar's-inkle."—Inkle was a form of inferior linen tape sold by pedlars and beggars (hence "beggars-inkle") going through the country districts. It resembled except in colour the red tape of public offices. About four miles from Cookstown, near Tullyhogue, Skerrygroom Factory, said to be Ireland's only tapeworks, was burned down in 1913. Several pieces of inkle were formerly woven in the same loom, and the looms were narrow and close together, with the result that a large number, with those working them, could be placed in the one room. Hence arose the phrase "As thick or as grate (friendly and intimate) as inkle-weavers." Compare "A Winter's Tale," IV., iv., 208—

"He hath ribbons of all the colours i' the rainbow . . . inkles, caddisses, cambrics, launs."

"Larn," learn, to teach.—"I'll larn ye to behave." Compare "Romeo and Juliet," III., ii., 12—

"Learn me how to lose a winning match."

"Lone," unmarried, single or widowed.—"She's a lone girl" or "A lone woman."
In the "Title Collect. Records" of 1642 there is a reference to "Queen Elizabeth being a lone woman and having few friends, refusing to marry." Compare "Henry IV.," Part II., II., i., 35, where Mistress Quickly, the hostess of a tavern, says, "A hundred mark is a long one for a poor lone woman to bear."

"Mitch" or "Mich," to play truant from school, as "He miched (or mitched) from school yesterday." Compare "Henry IV.," Part I., II., iv., 375—

"Shall the blessed son of heaven prove a micher and eat blackberries?"

(Mitch or miche is from the old French muchier, mucier, to hide, also to skulk, lurk.) In addition to mitch, mich, the word mooch or mouch—apparently from the same origin (old French muchier, to hide or skulk)—is used in the North of Ireland in the sense of idling or loafing with the idea of pilfering. "Watch yon boy mouchin' about the house; he's after no good."

In Certain English Dialects

(not, however, in Ulster) mouch is used with the idea to play truant in order to gather blackberries, and in Gloucestershire and Devonshire mooch is employed as meaning a blackberry. It is interesting to note that in the fifteenth and seventeenth centuries mich and mouch were used largely in the central counties of England in the same way, and especially with the idea of playing truant to gather blackberries. The words on coming to Ulster became slightly altered in their meaning (as explained) in our dialect.

"North," cold, indifferent, freezing, unfriendly.—"He gave him the north side of his countenance" (that is, there was a chilliness in the way he received him). Compare "Twelfth Night," III, ii., 23—

"You are now sailed into the north of my lady's opinion."

"Overlook," to bewitch, to look with the evil eye.—"The cows won't give milk, for the man that was here yesterday overlooked them." Compare "Merry Wives of Windsor," V., v., 80, where Pistol says to Falstaff—

"Vile worm thou wast o'erlook'd even in thy birth;"

and "The Merchant of Venice," III., ii., 15, where Portia says:—

Shakespeare and the Ulster Dialect

"Beshrew your eyes,
They have o'erlook'd me."

"Blink" is also used for "overlook."

"Pick-thank," one who "picks a thank"—that is, curries favour with another, especially by informing against someone else; hence a flatterer or tale-bearer or mischief-maker. "He's an oul pick-thank." This word is used in Cavan and in the North-West of Ulster (compare MacManus's "Silk of Kine"), and in the dialects of Warwickshire, Worcestershire, Devonshire, and Gloucestershire. See "Henry IV.," Part I., III., ii.. 23—

"Many tales devised,
Which oft the ear of greatness needs must hear,
By smiling pick-thanks and base news-mongers."

In Cavan another name for a pick-thank is a "packet-carrier" or a "levet-carrier."

"Posy."—If an Ulster country girl is asked what she is carrying she will answer, whether it is a single flower or a bunch of flowers, "A posy." This is a shortened form of poesy, which even when written in full was often pronounced in two syllables. The word was used—(1) For a short motto, originally a line or verse of poetry inscribed on a knife or within a ring. In "The Merchant of Venice," V., i., 147, we read—

"A ring . . . whose posy was,
  For all the world like cutlers' poetry
  Upon a knife: 'Love me and leave me not,' "

and in the old song of "Giles Scroggins' Ghost"—

"He bought a ring with this posy true,
  If you loves I as I loves you—
  No knife shall cut our lives in two."

(2) It was employed for an emblem or emblematic device. (3) Finally, probably from the custom of combining flowers so as to form a significant expression, for a bunch of flowers, nosegay, or bouquet. This use of the word is now dialectal, yet in 1593 in one of Marlowe's works, we find it employed—

"And I will make thee beds of roses
  And a thousand fragrant posies."

Probably Shakespeare borrowed the phrase from Marlowe, for in the "Merry Wives of Windsor," III., i., 17, Evans says to Simple—

"There will we make our beds of roses
  And a thousand fragrant posies."

Compare also—

"He promised he'd bring me a basket of posies,
  A garland of lilies, a garland of roses,

Shakespeare and the Ulster Dialect

A little straw hat to set off the blue ribbons
That tie up my bonny brown hair."

(Old English Song.)

Many of the Elizabethan Writers,

and notably Shakespeare, were fond of punning (the most terrible pun in his plays occurs when Lady Macbeth—II., ii., 56—as she ascends the stairs to the chamber where the King lies murdered by her husband, utters the horrible jest—

"If he do bleed,
I'll gild the faces of the grooms withal,
For it must seem their guilt")

and of using a play upon words, and in the North of Ireland this type of literary expression has entered into the dialect of the people, as the following sayings and proverbial expressions demonstrate:— "Rue and thyme makes a purty posy" (said when during a matrimonial engagement either party revokes); "Airly (early) risin' is the first thing that puts a man to the dur (door);" "Sit fast's a bad weed;" "She's a helpless body who has no shift" (compare "Cymbeline," I., ii., 1, "Sir, I would advise you to shift a shirt"); "Slips are (allowed) in dancing;" "Well laid, as the hen said" (a remark made when a man who is carrying a heavy sack of potatoes, &c., deposits it in the exact position where it is to be placed); "Kissing goes by favour."

"Puke."—This word is used in Ulster in three ways—(1) To vomit, hence mothers often say to the doctor when bringing their children to hospital, "Sir, saving yer presence, this chile of mine's always pukin'." Compare "As You Like It," II., vii., 140—

"The infant mewling and puking in the nurse's arms."

Shakespeare was the first writer to use the word in 1600, and he employs it only once, though the word "pukishness" is found (Oxford Dictionary) in 1581. (2) As an emetic. "Doctor, could you give me a puke to put my brother off the drink?" (3) As a term for a conceited, vain, and often unhealthy-looking person, who so disgusts people that at the sight of him they are inclined (as is not unusual on experiencing a foul odour) to expectorate and to say, "Oh, there's that puke!" It is a curious thing that puke is used in America for a native of Missouri. The early Californians christened as "pukes"—the word probably coming with the North of Ireland emigrants—the immigrants from Missouri, declaring that they had been vomited forth from that prolific State (Thornton's "An American Glossary," Vol. II., p. 707). In Haliburton's "Clockmaker" he refers to "the suckers of Illinoy, the pukes of Missouri, and the corncrakers of Virginia."

"Scantling," a small portion or sample. "That's a brave wee scantlin' of a pig," "I'll just take a scantlin' of bacon for breakfast." Compare "Troilus and Cressida," I., iii., 348—

"The success,
Although particular, shall give a scantling
Of good or bad unto the general."

"Skillet," a cooking utensil often made of brass or copper, with a long handle, and sometimes with three or four feet, used for boiling jam, making porridge, or stewing meat. (Its derivation is doubtful, but the source of the word may be Anglo-French or old French.) Compare "Othello," I., iii., 271—

"Let housewives make a skillet of my helm."

"Savin' yer presence" is an apologetic statement made by anyone when something disagreeable has to be said, as when a doctor is told an unpleasant fact about a patient this introductory statement is made. It means "With all respect to you," or "Except in your presence." It is probably another form of the

Phrase Used in "The Merchant of Venice,"

II., ii., 21—"I should be ruled by the fiend who, saving your reverence, is the devil himself." Probably "sir reverence," alteration of save (abbreviated to sa') reverence, "with all respect for," "with apologies to," is the same as used in "The Comedy of Errors," III., ii., 91—

"A very referent body; I such a one as a man may not speak of without he say 'Sir reverence.' "

Shakespeare and the Ulster Dialect

"Your reverence," a respectful form of address used in Ulster in speaking to a clergyman, is employed by Shakespeare in "Henry V.," I., ii., 20—

"For God doth know, how many, now in health,
Shall drop their blood in approbation
Of what your reverence shall incite us to:"

this is spoken by the King to the Archbishop of Canterbury. Compare also the Ulster couplet—

"Patience and perseverence
Got a wife for his reverence."

"Think long," to long for. An Ulster boy or girl writes home from school that he or she is "thinking long," meaning longing for home and relatives. In "A Song of Glenann" Moira O'Neill writes—

"An' now we're quarely betther fixed,
In troth, there's nothing wrong:
But me and mine, by rain an' shine,
We do be thinkin' long."

Compare "Romeo and Juliet," IV., v., 46, where in the tragic scene in which Juliet is found dead, Paris exclaims—

"Have I thought long to see this morning's face,
And doth it give me such a sight as this?"

"Trencherman," one with a good healthy appetite. "He's a great trencherman." Compare "Much Ado About Nothing," I., i., 51—

"He is a very valiant trencherman; he hath an excellent stomach."

This phrase is used only once by Shakespeare, but it is found in Sidney's "Arcadia."

"Wit," sense, intelligence. "He has his wit yet to seek" (he's a fool), "Would you even yer wit to the likes of him." Compare "Cymbeline," I., ii., 27—

"She's a good sign, but I have seen small reflection of her wit,"

and "The Two Gentlemen of Verona," III., i., 262—

"I am but a fool, look you; and yet I have the wit to think my master is a kind of knave."

These illustrations, which are only samples from a large collection, indicate in some degree what we owe in the North of Ireland to the same language which Shakespeare used as no other writer has ever done either before or since his days. It is one factor in the rich and varied Ulster dialect which to those who have the time and inclination for study and research is a most interesting and profitable occupation from

Shakespeare and the Ulster Dialect

the great light it throws upon history, philology, ethnography, and folk-lore.

[Reprinted from the "Northern Whig," 22nd April, 1916.]

www.ingramcontent.com/pod-product-compliance
Lightning Source LLC
Chambersburg PA
CBHW031508040426
42444CB00007B/1262